THE
TORTILLA
COOKBOOK

60 quick & easy, delicious wrap-based recipes
inspired by the world-famous challenge

SARAH COOK

SEVEN DIALS

First published in Great Britain in 2021 by Seven Dials,
an imprint of The Orion Publishing Group Ltd
Carmelite House, 50 Victoria Embankment
London EC4Y 0DZ

An Hachette UK Company

1 3 5 7 9 10 8 6 4 2

Photographer: Andrew Hayes-Watkins
Art Director and Design: Clare Sivell

A CIP catalogue record for this book is
available from the British Library.

ISBN (Hardback) 978 1 841885445
ISBN (eBook) 978 1 841885452

Printed and bound by DZS Grafik, d.o.o.

MIX
Paper from
responsible sources
FSC® C106600

www.orionbooks.co.uk

THE
TORTILLA
COOKBOOK

INTRODUCTION

First it was banana bread, then whipped iced coffee, but TikTok's greatest contribution to the food world may be the most useful one yet: the tortilla hack. A trick that first gained attention as a quick fix to the lockdown lunch rut has fast become the smartest way to fill a tortilla. The #tortillachallenge – a hashtag that collected billions of views in only a few short weeks – is no viral flash in the pan (pun intended). It is, quite simply, the tastiest, most effortless way to enjoy a wrap.

The concept is easy. Cut a slit to the centre of a tortilla, divide and fill sections with your favourite ingredients, then cleverly fold it all up to a neat, layered wedge that can be eaten as is or toasted until crispy. The result is a wonderfully portable sandwich that gives you the perfect combination of flavours and textures with every single bite.

There are endless variations to try, including speedy breakfast solutions, modern cheese toasties and plenty of veggie and vegan favourites. From the more traditional, Mexican-inspired fillings to classic British mash-ups, healthy Asian flavours and Mediterranean twists, there's even a chapter devoted entirely to sweet delights. In fact, once you've tried our Salted Caramel Banana Bread, you may never bother with the original again!

We've given you all the tools and tips you'll need to master this most-loved viral sensation and customise your own creations, plus lots more clever hacks that will transform your tortilla game forever. And if you're looking for a quick fix when you've got no fresh food in the house, check out the storecupboard-friendly recipes marked with a tin, like this ▯.

So, whether you're looking to reinvent your usual supper standbys, a tasty way to use up leftovers, something kid-friendly, or simply some grown-up indulgence, we've got you covered.

CHOOSE YOUR TORTILLA

WHEAT

Made from white or wholemeal flour, plus a little bit of fat which makes them super supple for wrapping, rolling and, of course, folding. They don't have the same depth of flavour that a corn base brings, but where some say bland, we say perfectly neutral so they're ideal for all sorts of weird and wacky fillings. Then there's that all-important elasticity which you only get with wheat, meaning they can come in some pretty huge sizes compared to their more fragile corny counterparts – and who wouldn't want to supersize their sandwich if they could. Ready-made varieties are available in white, wholewheat, half & half, or with the added health benefits of multigrain or seeded. And whatever type you choose, once warmed you can enjoy soft, stretchy tortillas that shouldn't break no matter what you cram inside them.

CORN

Good, pure corn tortillas have a lovely nutty, sweet corn flavour and are naturally wheat-free, but this lack of gluten, and any fat, also makes them a lot less flexible, even once warmed. This explains why they're usually fairly small, as a corn tortilla made too large would almost certainly fall apart when generously stuffed. Traditionally, you can choose between yellow, white or blue corn (yes, really), but it's also worth trying the relatively new, wheat–corn blend tortillas which are a lot less brittle than their whole corn cousins, but also have a decent flavour.

FLAVOURED

Switch things up with a tasty twist on the classic. Many wraps have popular flavours added for increased colour and appeal, like sweet chilli, buttery brioche and spinach. Others are designed to have lower carbs or appeal to allergy sufferers, substituting a significant portion of the usual base ingredients for vegetables like beetroot and cauliflower.

GLUTEN-FREE

Some tortilla wraps contain other wholegrain flours like rice, quinoa and teff to replicate the qualities of regular wheat-based tortillas. Others blend nut or coconut flours, and even sweet potato into wheat-free versions which can be delicious but are often heavily flavoured, so best suited to certain sandwich fillings over others. Look out for the 'GF' symbol on the recipes which are gluten-free friendly.

MAKING THE TORTILLA

For handheld, mess-free (and completely customisable) tortilla sandwiches and toasties, just follow these simple steps.

FILLING

1. Start with a suitably sized tortilla and make a slit from the edge nearest to you into the centre – kitchen scissors make the job easy. Imagine the wrap being divided into four (or sometimes three) sections with different ingredients to be added into each.

2. Place the first filling in the bottom left quarter (or third) – something creamy, saucy or sticky works well here so it doesn't fall off when folding over.

3. Add something like protein in the next quarter, say chicken, beans or egg, that will absorb the flavours from the first section. Or if toasting, this is the place to put anything you don't want to overcook, for example salady stuff like lettuce and cucumber, because it will be 'wrapped' up in the other fillings.

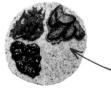

4. The next section will be in contact with your pan or press if toasting, so something you want warmed works nicely here. Otherwise anything crumbled, chopped or shredded will be safely sealed in here.

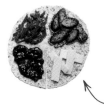

5. For hot wraps, finish the last section with cheese. As this is another outer layer it'll melt perfectly and become the 'glue' that will stick your wrap together. If enjoying cold, then use slices or sticky stuff preferably – anything too itty bitty risks spilling out when eating.

FOLDING

6. Fold the wrap, starting from the bottom left quarter (or third), and folding this first section up and over the second.

7. Fold the second section carefully over the third.

8. Finish by folding the wrap down to enclose the final section so you have a triangular wedge. Quarters will give you a smaller, fatter triangle; thirds a flatter, wider triangle.

HOW TO COOK

Go low and slow for heftier fillings that need more warming or melting time. Hot and fast is the answer when you want the tortilla to crisp up quickly as the ingredients inside don't need much cooking time; this works for oozy things likely to flood out and fill your pan instead of your sandwich. Cream cheeses, crème fraîche, marshmallows and sauces like chocolate and caramel are good examples. Also, unless well chilled, runny cheeses fall into this category, too.

FEEDING FAMILY AND FRIENDS

Although our wrap recipes are perfectly portioned for one, if you're serving without any sides you might want a couple for dinner. On all other occasions, a single tortilla stack should satisfy, and you've always got the option to go large.

When you're catering for a crowd, though, it's worth setting up a conveyor belt of tortillas for cutting, filling and folding, and unless you've got an industrial-sized sandwich press, you'll probably only be able to cook two to four wraps at the same time. Instead, have an oven on low (about 100°C/200°F) and keep the already filled and toasted wraps warm, covered loosely with foil to prevent drying out, while you toast extra batches.

TOP TEN TORTILLA HACKS

1. **No sandwich press? No problem.** While you're assembling your tortilla, throw two frying pans onto your hob to heat up. Add your sandwich to the largest pan, pop the smaller frying pan on top and add your heaviest saucepan or casserole on top of that. Cook until crisp and toasted. (Just make sure the bases of your pans are clean!)

2. **Got a sandwich press but never use it?** Bacon, chorizo slices, halloumi and paneer all fry up perfectly, or fake roasted veg by charring onion, aubergine, courgette and pepper pieces in minutes.
3. **A waffle iron makes a great impromptu sandwich press, but a regular iron is just as good.** Wrap your sandwich in baking parchment, heat your iron to its highest setting and, hey presto, lunch and laundry.
4. **Batch-assemble wraps for quick lunches, saving time and food waste.** Fill them with anything that can be frozen (basically steer clear of raw veg and salad leaves), then fold up and freeze. Grab from your freezer at breakfast time and by lunchtime you're ready to toast.
5. **Pre-grated cheese** – good for usability, bad for use-by dates. Rather than risk losing it to the bin, spread it on a tray and open-freeze. Once solid, tip into an airtight container and sprinkle frozen cheese straight onto your tortilla. (Keeps well for a couple of months.)
6. **Wrap too stale to wrap up?** Pop it in the microwave with a damp paper towel on top and cook on High power for 30 seconds.
7. **Or don't let them get to the stale stage.** Once you've opened a pack of tortillas, freeze them, stacked between sheets of greaseproof paper or baking parchment so you can easily remove just one at a time.
8. **Avoid cracking corn tortillas by 'steaming' first to soften.** Sounds fancy, but simply dip them quickly in water before tossing in a hot frying pan for a few seconds on each side.
9. **Love lunch, hate dishes?** Wrap your folded tortillas in baking parchment before putting into your sandwich press. No leaks, no mess, no washing up.
10. **Add a tortilla to your box of home-made cookies** – the moisture in the tortilla will keep the cookies soft and chewy and stop them drying out and getting stale. Worth wasting a wrap for, we reckon.

PIMP YOUR WRAP

Ready-made tortillas might lack the toasty depth of flavour you'd get from freshly made, but what you lose in taste you gain in shelf life, as unopened packs can sit happily for months, making great mealtime standbys. And here's our pick of the best long-life store-cupboard supplies to keep handy, for adding oompf to boring fridge fare when lunch is looking lousy.

Pesto really packs a flavour punch. Open a jar and sort dinner at the same time.

Crispy fried onions add crunch to salads, authenticity to Asian flavours, and depth to cheese toasties.

Canned chickpeas make easy, instant hummus. Just tip the whole can, liquid and all, into your food processor with 2 tablespoons lemon juice and 2 teaspoons ground cumin. Blitz until super-smooth and season.

Good, plain mayo is the ideal, neutrally flavoured 'glue' for a folded wrap that won't spill its fillings. Or jazz it up with crushed garlic, mustard, chipotle paste or lemon zest.

Mango chutney might not be your favourite pickle, but what else pairs brilliantly with bhajis, baltis, Bombay potatoes *and* good old ham and cheese?

Sundried tomatoes are the salad you can keep in your cupboard. Great for when there's not so much as a wilted lettuce leaf to be had.

Chilli sauce for marinating, dressing, drizzling and dunking. Choose your favourite, whether that's sweet and sticky, or knock-your-socks-off fiery.

Tuna is the perfect filler for when the fridge is bare, and small tins are the perfect portion size for one regular wrap.

Marinated artichokes for veggies, vegans and anyone else who hates tuna.

Burger pickles, cornichons, gherkins – whatever tickles your pickle. Just as good with Scandi-style salmon as they are with cheeseburgers. **Tomato purée** lasts forever (just about) but makes pizza possible in minutes.

Peanut butter (or your preferred nut butter). Perfect for sweet combos with chocolate, jam or banana, as well as savoury satay flavours.

Salted caramel sauce. Forget microwave mug cakes – still too much effort. The really instant pudding is a tortilla with some sticky caramel sauce and just about anything else. Caramel and peanut butter? I think so. Caramel and fruit? Good. Caramel and chocolate? Yes. Caramel and cake? Hell, yes.

Any (or all) of our other favourite flavour-makers, like **mustard, miso, tahini, olives, onion chutney, barbecue sauce** and **mint sauce**.

And remember, the storecupboard-friendly recipes are marked with a tin, like this 🥫.

BREAKFAST
& BRUNCH

Boston baked beans

A favourite American dish that works perfectly when deconstructed, covered in cheese and wrapped in a crispy tortilla.

1 tortilla (try a large, soft white flour wrap or gluten-free alternative)

1–2 tablespoons barbecue sauce

2–3 cooked smoked streaky bacon rashers

2 tablespoons baked beans

a few slices or a small handful of grated Cheddar or Monterey Jack

a few thin slices of red onion

knob of butter, for frying (optional)

Cut your tortilla from the edge nearest to you into the centre, then assemble as follows.

bottom left Spread over the barbecue sauce.

top left Snap the bacon into a few pieces and cover as much of the section as you can.

top right Use a fork to roughly crush half of the beans, then stir back into the rest and spread them over.

bottom right Toss together the cheese and onion and press onto the last quarter of the tortilla.

Fold up the tortilla from the bottom left corner clockwise around the wrap. Carefully lift into a hot frying pan and fry for 1–2 minutes on each side until golden and crisp – you might want to add a knob of butter. Make sure the beans are hot – if not, turn the heat down, cover the pan and leave for a few more minutes.

MAKE IT VEGGIE
Swap the bacon for strips of a whole ready-roasted red pepper, and sprinkle the beans with sweet smoked paprika to replicate that smoky taste.

Scrambled eggs Florentine

V GF

Adding a dollop of hollandaise to the scrambled eggs makes them extra creamy.

2 eggs
1 heaped tablespoon
snipped chives
large knob of butter
3 heaped tablespoons
ready-made
hollandaise sauce
1 tortilla (try a regular,
soft white flour wrap
or gluten-free
alternative)
1 small handful of baby
spinach
salt and freshly ground
black pepper

Whisk the eggs with the chives and a little salt and roughly whisk. Melt the butter in a pan then add the eggs and scramble over a low heat. When the eggs are almost ready, stir through 1 heaped tablespoon of hollandaise sauce. Quickly warm the tortilla according to the packet instructions, and make a cut from the edge nearest to you into the centre. Follow the order of toppings below.

bottom left Spoon on half the scrambled eggs and season with some pepper.

top left Warm the remaining hollandaise and spread half of it over, then top with half the spinach.

top right Spoon on the remaining scrambled eggs and season with some pepper.

bottom right Spread over the remaining hollandaise, then top with the rest of the spinach.

Fold up the tortilla from the bottom left corner clockwise around the wrap. Enjoy straightaway.

> **WHY NOT TRY?**
> Making it eggs Royale by swapping half the spinach for some smoked salmon, or some ham for eggs Benedict.

Scandi-salmon

A classic that is fresh, flavourful and very flexible – you could swap the shallot for onion, capers for caper berries, cucumber for thinly sliced fennel, and even the salmon for hot-smoked trout.

1 tortilla (try a seeded wrap, beetroot-flavoured, or gluten-free alternative)
2 3 tablespoons cream cheese
1 round shallot, diced
1 teaspoon small capers, rinsed
2 cornichons, thinly sliced
2 slices of smoked salmon
freshly ground black pepper
finger-length chunk of cucumber, very finely sliced
lemon wedge
sprig of dill (optional)

Warm the tortilla according to the packet instructions, then make a cut from the edge nearest to you into the centre. Follow the order of toppings below.

bottom left Generously spread with the cream cheese.

top left Toss together the diced shallot, capers and sliced cornichons and scatter over.

top right Add the salmon with some black pepper.

bottom right Add the cucumber slices and season with a squeeze of lemon juice and some feathery dill fronds, if using (discard the thicker dill stem).

Fold up the tortilla from the bottom left corner clockwise around the wrap, and enjoy.

> **WHY NOT TRY?**
> Cutting the calories by swapping the cream cheese for cottage cheese.

Corn & smashed avocado

(V) (GF)

An Antipodean-style brunch – just don't forget the Bloody Marys.

1 tortilla (try a corn
    wrap or gluten-free
    alternative)
1 small, ripe avocado
salt and freshly ground
    black pepper
juice of ½ lime
115–140g (4–5oz) tin
    sweetcorn (depending
    on tortilla size),
    drained well
85–115g (3–4oz) feta
½ teaspoon cumin seeds,
    preferably toasted

Prepare the tortilla by cutting from the edge nearest to you into the centre, then assemble as follows.

bottom left Mash the flesh of the avocado with plenty of seasoning and lots of lime juice, then spread over the first section of tortilla.

top Scatter over the sweetcorn.

bottom right Finely crumble the feta, toss with the cumin seeds and spread over the remaining tortilla.

Fold up the tortilla from the bottom left section clockwise around the wrap. Push back in any sweetcorn that escapes, then use a sandwich press to toast, or cook in a hot frying pan for 1–2 minutes on each side until golden and crisp.

> **WHY NOT TRY?**
> Spicing it up. Add splashes of Tabasco, pinches of dried chilli flakes, or even diced fresh chilli to the smashed avocado.

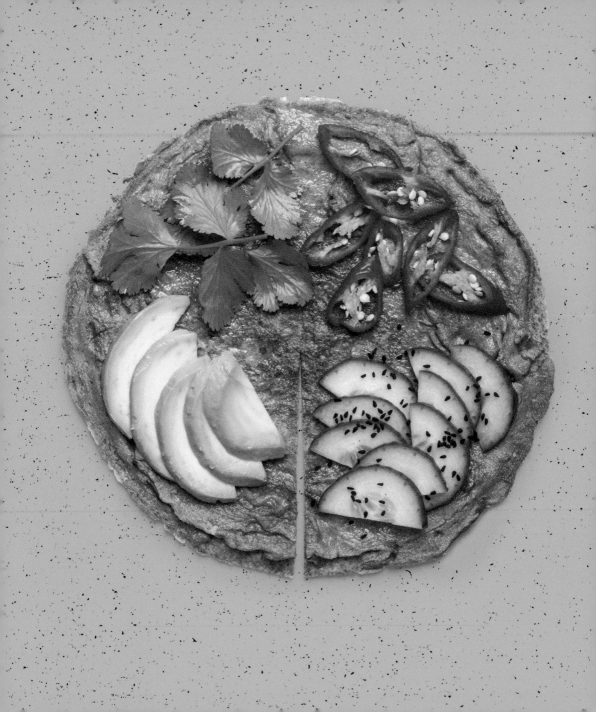

Indian egg wrap

(V) (GF)

Inspired by a Kolkata egg roll, where a thin 'omelette' is cooked onto a paratha.

1 egg
¼ teaspoon each turmeric and mild curry powder
1 large tortilla (try a medium wholewheat wrap or gluten-free alternative)
½ ripe avocado, peeled and sliced
2 lemon wedges
few sprigs of coriander
1 fresh red or green chilli, finely sliced (seeds left in if you like it really spicy)
few slices of cucumber
a pinch of nigella seeds

Whisk the egg with the turmeric and curry powder plus a pinch of salt. Heat a good glug of mild oil in a non-stick or cast-iron frying pan. Moving very fast, tip in the egg and immediately press the tortilla on top. Move the tortilla around to cover it completely in the egg. Cook for a few more seconds until set, then flip to briefly warm the other side. Tip onto a chopping board, egg-side up, and cut into the centre from the edge nearest you, then follow the order of toppings below.

bottom left Arrange the avocado slices and squeeze over some lemon juice.

top left Add whole sprigs of coriander, or just the leaves.

top right Sprinkle over as much fresh chilli as you like.

bottom right Arrange the cucumber slices then scatter with the nigella seeds.

Fold up the tortilla from the bottom left corner clockwise around the wrap. Squeeze over a little more lemon juice, if you like.

WHY NOT TRY?
Filling with almost anything once you've got the technique: crunchy salad veg, leftover meat or daal.

Bacon-banana waffle stack

Trust us, this is the ultimate in sweet–salty pairings.

1 tortilla (try a large, soft white flour wrap)
glug of maple syrup, plus extra to serve
1 ready-made sweet toasting waffle, lightly toasted
2–3 cooked smoked streaky bacon rashers or pancetta slices
½ ripe banana, thinly sliced
large knob of butter

Prepare the tortilla by cutting from the edge nearest to you into the centre, then assemble as follows.

bottom left Drizzle over some maple syrup.

top left Add the waffle.

top right Cover the section with bacon or pancetta slices.

bottom right Fan out the banana slices.

Fold up the tortilla from the bottom left corner clockwise around the wrap, and squish with your hand to firmly stick the fillings in place. Use a sandwich press to toast, or cook in a hot frying pan with a knob of butter for 2 minutes on each side, until the tortilla is golden and crisp. Serve with lots of extra maple syrup.

MAKE IT VEGGIE OR VEGAN
Use a vegetarian or vegan waffle and swap the bacon for toasted walnuts.

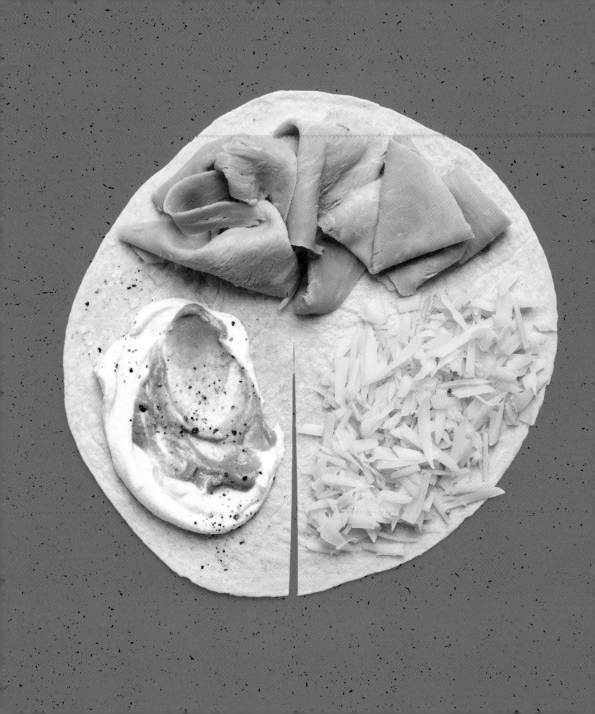

Croque monsieur

Traditionally made with a béchamel sauce, this quick and easy cheat involves just a dollop of crème fraîche instead.

1 tortilla (try a regular, soft white flour wrap or gluten-free alternative)
2 tablespoons crème fraîche
1–2 teaspoons Dijon mustard
2–3 wafer-thin slices of smoked ham
salt and freshly ground black pepper
large handful of grated Gruyère or Emmental

Cut the tortilla from the edge nearest to you into the centre, then assemble as follows.

bottom left Mix together the crème fraîche, mustard, some salt and pepper, and spread over.

top Ruffle up the ham to fill the top section of the tortilla.

bottom right Sprinkle over the cheese.

Fold up the tortilla from the bottom left section clockwise around the wrap. Use a sandwich press to toast, or cook in a hot frying pan for 2 minutes on each side until the cheese is melted.

WHY NOT TRY?
A croque madame: top your toastie with a fried egg.

Tex-Med toastie

If you have any coriander left over, it would make a welcome addition here.

Some leftover cooked sweet potato – a spoon of mash, half a jacket or a few chunks of roasted
30g (1oz) chorizo chunk, finely sliced, or 4 slices salami-style chorizo
1 tortilla (try a corn wrap or gluten-free alternative, like sweet potato)
200g (7oz) tin black beans, drained and rinsed
salt and freshly ground black pepper
55–75g (2–2½oz) feta, crumbled
small handful of grated Cheddar
1 spring onion, finely sliced

Add the chorizo slices to a cold frying pan big enough to fit the tortilla. Cook over a low–medium heat until the slices are just crisping on both sides, then remove with a slotted spoon, leaving the oil in the pan.

Cut the tortilla from the edge nearest to you into the centre and assemble as follows.

bottom left Tip on the beans, crush with a fork and season.

top Add the sweet potato and use a fork to mash directly onto the tortilla. Top with the chorizo slices.

bottom right Toss together the feta and Cheddar with the spring onion and press onto the final section.

Fold up the tortilla from the bottom left section clockwise around the wrap, then return to the frying pan of chorizo oil and cook over a medium heat for 1–2 minutes on each side until the outside is crispy and the fillings hot.

GOOD WITH some cool yogurt for dunking 'Tex' style, or tzatziki for 'Med' style.

BBQ pork stack

Eat with jalapeños if you like it spicy, or gherkins if you like it sweeter.

1 tortilla (try a corn and wheat wrap or gluten-free alternative)
handful of shredded ham hock (or 1 thick slice, torn up)
3 tablespoons barbecue sauce
1 tablespoon tomato purée
a little ready-made coleslaw
1 ready-made hash brown (gluten-free if needed), cooked following packet instructions
55g (2oz) mature Cheddar, sliced

Warm the tortilla following the packet instructions so it's soft enough to wrap around these chunky fillings without splitting. Cut the tortilla from edge nearest to you into the centre. Assemble as follows.

bottom left Mix the ham hock well with the barbecue sauce and tomato purée. Pile on.

top left Spread over a thin layer of the coleslaw.

top right Top with the cooked hash brown.

bottom right Finish with the cheese slices.

Carefully fold up the tortilla from the bottom left corner clockwise around the wrap. Use a sandwich press to toast, or heat in a hot frying pan for 1–2 minutes on each side until the tortilla is golden on the outside. Eat straightaway.

> **MAKE IT VEGGIE**
> Swap the ham hock for tinned jackfruit.

EVERYDAY
FAVOURITES

Simple beef taco

(GF)

This solo number is easily transformed into a full family feast – just cook up the whole sachet of spice mix with a whole pack of minced beef, and scale up the other fillings. A mild Cheddar makes a good substitute for the Red Leicester.

1 tortilla (try a corn wrap or gluten-free alternative)
55g (2oz) minced beef
2 teaspoons fajita spice mix
1–2 tablespoons mild or hot tomato salsa
small handful of shredded iceberg or cos lettuce
handful of grated Red Leicester or Colby cheese

Cut the tortilla from the edge nearest to you into the centre. Cook the mince in a frying pan over a medium heat for few minutes and break it up a little. When browned, add the fajita spice mix and fry for a couple more minutes, then assemble the tortilla as follows.

bottom left Spread some salsa over the tortilla, but don't go right to the edges. You can always serve the tortilla with extra salsa, so don't overfill here or you'll risk losing it when toasting.

top left Add the shredded lettuce and pat down.

top right Spoon on the hot, spicy mince.

bottom right Pile on the grated cheese and squash down.

Fold up the tortilla from the bottom left corner clockwise around the wrap. Use a sandwich press to toast, or heat in a hot frying pan for 2 minutes on each side until the tortilla is golden and crisp and the cheese has melted. Serve with extra salsa.

> **MAKE IT VEGGIE**
> Simply use meat-free mince in place of the beef.

Brilliant BLT

(GF)

A classic made lighter by using a seeded tortilla (which means you can eat two).

1 tortilla (try a seeded wrap or gluten-free alternative)
1 heaped tablespoon aioli or garlic mayonnaise
small handful of torn lettuce or spinach leaves
1–2 cooked smoked streaky or back bacon rashers
a few slices of tomato
freshly ground black pepper

Cut the tortilla from the edge nearest to you into the centre. Add the fillings as follows.

bottom left Spread with the aioli or mayo.

top left Squash down the lettuce or spinach leaves.

top right Snap the bacon into a few pieces and cover as much of the section as you can.

bottom right Add the tomato slices and season with lots of freshly ground black pepper.

Fold up the tortilla from the bottom left corner clockwise around the wrap.

WHY NOT TRY?
Upgrading to a BLAT with an avocado layer. Use a fork to smash a little into the top left area before adding the rest of your greenery.

Fuss-free quesadilla

No flipping, just folding. A simple supper just became even simpler.

1 tortilla (try a regular, soft white flour wrap or gluten-free alternative)
a big spoon of tinned refried beans
3–4 heaped tablespoons sweetcorn, tinned or frozen
1 spring onion, shredded
good handful of grated Cheddar or Monterey Jack

Cut the tortilla from the edge nearest to you into the centre. Assemble as follows.

bottom left Warm the beans in a microwave or pan, beating with a spoon to loosen them, then spread over the section.

top left Add the sweetcorn.

top right Spread out the shredded spring onion.

bottom right Pile on the grated cheese.

Fold up the tortilla from the bottom left corner clockwise around the wrap. Use a sandwich press to toast, or heat in a hot frying pan for 1–2 minutes on each side until golden. Eat straightaway with your favourite Tex-Mex dips and salsas for dunking.

MAKE IT VEGAN
Use your favourite Cheddar substitute.

Italian tuna & white bean

A little more effort in the making is balanced by the fact that most of these ingredients will already be lurking on your kitchen shelves.

1 tortilla (try a wholewheat wrap or gluten-free alternative)

1 garlic clove, finely grated or crushed

2 teaspoons extra virgin olive oil

1 teaspoon white wine vinegar

1 teaspoon Dijon mustard

salt and freshly ground black pepper

¼ tin of white beans (cannellini, haricot or butter are all good), drained and rinsed

1 x roughly 80g (3oz) tin tuna, well drained

large handful of salad leaves

a few sundried tomatoes, or a few cherry or small plum tomatoes, sliced

If you like, warm the tortilla according to the packet instructions, then cut from the edge nearest to you into the centre, and add the toppings as follows.

bottom left Put the garlic, oil, vinegar and mustard into a small mixing bowl with some seasoning and mix with a fork to make a creamy dressing. Add the beans, lightly crush into the dressing, then 'spread' over the tortilla section.

top left Flake the tuna over.

top right Add the salad leaves in an even layer.

bottom right Arrange the tomatoes and if using fresh ones, season with lots of freshly ground black pepper.

Fold up the tortilla from the bottom left corner clockwise around the wrap. Eat straightaway if you don't want a soggy bottom.

WHY NOT TRY?
Doubling up. The recipe makes a generous amount of dressing, so you could mix with half a tin of beans and save the rest for another sandwich or salad.

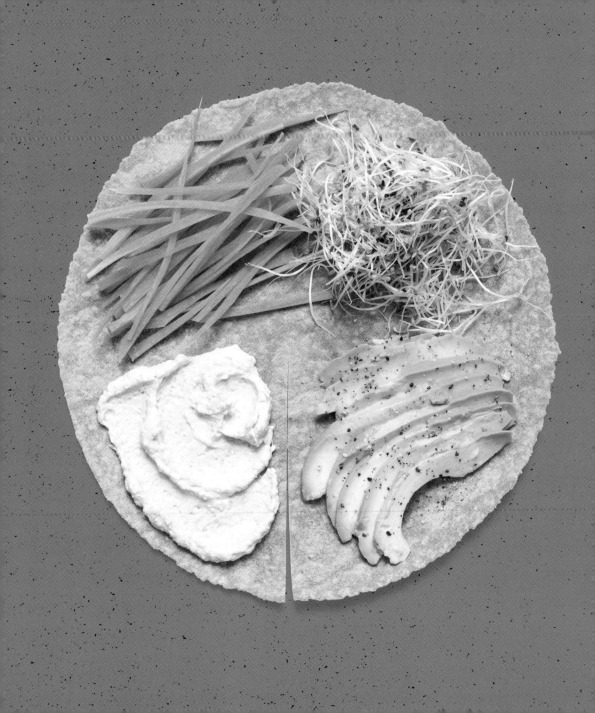

Bugs bunny

Packed with loads of fresh flavours, this vegan lunch wrap is super satisfying but knocked up in minutes.

1 tortilla (try a sweet potato wrap or gluten-free alternative)
2–3 tablespoons hummus (lemon & coriander is good)
1 small carrot
handful of alfafa sprouts
½ ripe avocado, peeled and thinly sliced
wedge of lemon or lime
salt and freshly ground black pepper

Cut the tortilla from the edge nearest to you into the centre. Add the fillings as follows.

bottom left Spread a good, thick layer of hummus.

top left After peeling, coarsely grate or slice the carrot into matchsticks with a julienne peeler. Pile onto the section.

top right Add your alfafa sprouts.

bottom right Dress the avocado slices with a squeeze of lemon or lime juice. Arrange over the final section and season well with salt and pepper.

Fold up the tortilla from the bottom left corner clockwise around the wrap, and eat immediately or pack into a lunchbox for later. This recipe travels well – keeping the hummus in the middle of the stack means your sarnies aren't soggy come lunchtime.

> **WHY NOT TRY?**
> Adding some spicy crunch with a sprinkling of dukkah, savoury granola or toasted seeds, such as pumpkin or linseed, and a squirt of hot chilli sauce.

Ham & sweet pea

This smacks of spring lunchtimes, when you're starting to crave lighter, brighter flavours.

1 tortilla (try a regular wholewheat wrap or gluten-free alternative)
55g (2oz) frozen peas or leftover cooked peas
salt and freshly ground black pepper
1–2 tablespoons piccalilli
large handful of shredded ham hock, or 2 slices of ham
small handful of lamb's lettuce

Warm the tortilla following the packet instructions, then cut from the edge nearest to you into the centre. If you're using frozen peas, cook these following the packet instructions too, then rinse under cold water to quickly cool and pat dry with kitchen paper. Add the fillings as described below.

bottom left Dice up any chunkier bits of veg in your piccalilli, then spread over this section.

top left Use a fork to lightly crush the peas onto the tortilla so they stick a little. Season with a little salt and pepper.

top right Add the ham.

bottom right Top with the lamb's lettuce.

Fold up the tortilla from the bottom left corner clockwise around the wrap.

> **GOOD WITH** a wedge of good cheese, a few pickled onions, some celery sticks and an apple. If you can't enjoy an al fresco Ploughman's, make one 'al desko'!

Toasted Club

An absolute classic is taken to the next level by using crunchy, crumbed chicken and some piquant pickles.

1 tortilla (try a large, soft white flour wrap)
1 heaped tablespoon mayonnaise or mustard mayonnaise
2 sandwich slices of sweet cucumber pickle or gherkin
1 cooked breaded chicken breast fillet (you'll use about half, so save the rest for a second sandwich)
1 round slice of red onion
1–2 slices of beef tomato
salt and freshly ground black pepper
2 slices of Swiss cheese, such as Gouda or Emmental
1 bacon rasher, cooked until crisp

Warm the tortilla according to the packet instructions (although you will be toasting it later, it needs to be nice and soft to pack in all of these fillings). Cut the tortilla from the edge nearest to you into the centre, then top as described below.

bottom left Spread over the mayo and top with the pickles.

top left Slice up the chicken breast to make it easier to neatly fill the section with as much as you can cram in.

top right Separate the onion slice into rings and space over the tortilla section before topping with the tomato.

bottom right Add the cheese then top with the bacon.

Fold up the tortilla from the bottom left corner clockwise around the wrap, then squash down with the palm of your hand to compress the stack. Use a sandwich press to toast, or cook in a hot frying pan for 1–2 minutes on each side until crispy.

GOOD WITH a pile of creamy coleslaw and some ready-salted crisps.

Veggie deli

Artichokes pair perfectly with the other flavours here, and make a 'meaty' filling for a vegetarian sandwich, but you could use up any deli veg you have going spare.

1 tortilla (try a seeded wrap or gluten-free alternative)
1 heaped tablespoon sundried tomato pesto
4 marinated artichoke hearts (or 8 halves), from a jar or tin
small handful of baby spinach leaves
large handful of ready-grated mozzarella mixed with grated Cheddar

Warm the tortilla according to the packet instructions, to make it nice and soft. Cut the tortilla from the edge nearest to you into the centre, then add the fillings as described below.

bottom left Spread with the pesto.

top left Pull apart the artichokes into thinner pieces and arrange to fill the section.

top right Add the spinach leaves.

bottom right Add the grated cheese mix.

Fold up the tortilla from the bottom left corner clockwise around the wrap, then squash the stack to flatten it a bit. Use a sandwich press to toast, or cook in a hot frying pan for 1–2 minutes on each side until the tortilla is crispy and the cheese has melted.

> **MAKE IT VEGAN**
> Use vegan pesto and your favourite mozzarella-style cheese substitute.

Fish finger foldie

Keep your freezer well-stocked – adding a waffle to anything makes it instantly better (and remember you can cook them in your toaster too . . .).

1 tortilla (try a large wholewheat wrap)
large dollop of ready-made tartare sauce or mayo
small handful of chopped crisp lettuce, such as baby gem or iceberg
2–3 frozen fish fingers, cooked following packet instructions
1 frozen potato waffle, cooked following packet instructions
large dollop of tomato ketchup

Gently warm the tortilla following the packet instructions, and make a cut from the edge nearest to you into the centre. Add the fillings as follows.

bottom left Spread over the tartare sauce or mayo. Add a smattering of lettuce – too much and you'll have trouble eating it!

top Roughly break up the hot fish fingers into chunks with a fork, and arrange over the section.

bottom right Add the waffle and top with a dollop of tomato ketchup – all the better for sticking the wrap together.

Fold up the tortilla from the bottom left section clockwise around the wrap.

WHY NOT TRY?
Pimping up the classic by using frozen scampi instead of those fish fingers.

Meatless marinara

Brunch, lunch or supper, this super 'sub'-stitute for that meaty favourite is delicious anytime. Plus you can freeze all of the leftover ingredients for a second round another day.

1 tortilla (try a seeded wrap or gluten-free alternative)
2–3 tablespoons tomato pasta sauce
4–5 cooked falafel
large handful of grated mozzarella (or ½ mozzarella ball, patted dry and grated)
salt and freshly ground black pepper

Cut the tortilla from the edge nearest to you into the centre, then add the fillings as described below.

bottom left Spread with an even layer of tomato pasta sauce.

top Crumble each falafel into a few pieces and use to fill the top section. Use a potato masher or the palm of your hand to squash them into a roughly flat layer.

bottom right Add the mozzarella and season with plenty of salt and pepper.

Fold up the tortilla from the bottom left section clockwise around the wrap. Use a sandwich press to toast, or cook in a hot frying pan for 2–3 minutes on each side until the fillings are heated through and the tortilla is really crispy.

> **MAKE IT VEGAN**
> Use a mozzarella-style cheese substitute. Most falafels are naturally vegan anyway, but always check the packet.

Portuguese sardine

 GF

This little riff on Portugal's speciality sardine pâté should transport you straight to a sunny beach, but as it's store-cupboard friendly you'll be able to make it all year round.

1 tortilla (try a regular, soft white flour wrap or gluten-free alternative)
1 tablespoon sundried tomato paste
4 sundried tomatoes from a jar, drained and sliced
1 x 120g (4oz) tin of sardines in olive oil (boneless or whole), drained
1 tablespoon mayonnaise
small handful of salad leaves or rocket

Prepare the tortilla by cutting from the side nearest to you into the centre, and then filling as follows.

bottom left Mix the tomato paste with a teaspoon of the herby oil from the sundried tomato jar and spread over the section.

top left Cover with the sardines.

top right Spread with the mayo, then scatter the sundried tomatoes evenly over the top.

bottom right Add the salad leaves.

Fold up the tortilla from the bottom left corner clockwise around the wrap.

> **WHY NOT TRY?**
> Swapping the sardines for tinned tuna, or even peppered smoked mackerel.

Instant pizza slice

If meat-feast is more your thing, swap the fried mushrooms for slices of salami.

large knob of butter or dairy-free spread
large handful of sliced mushrooms
salt
dried oregano
1 tortilla (try a large, soft white flour wrap or gluten-free alternative)
1 heaped tablespoon tomato pasta sauce, passata or tomato purée
small handful of olives (any type), stoned and sliced
a few slices of red onion
large handful of ready-grated mozzarella

Melt the butter or spread in a frying pan over a medium heat, and fry the mushrooms with a little salt for a few minutes. When soft and really golden, stir in a good sprinkle of dried oregano. Cut the tortilla from the edge nearest to you into the centre, then assemble as follows.

bottom left Use the back of a spoon to spread over your tomatoey choice. Scatter with the olives and onion slices.

top Add the cooked mushrooms.

bottom right Pack the cheese evenly over the section.

Fold up the tortilla from the bottom left section clockwise around the wrap. Use a sandwich press to toast, or cook in a frying pan over a low heat for 3–4 minutes on each side, until the cheese is oozing and the onion is softening. Enjoy!

> **MAKE IT VEGAN**
> Use a ready-grated mozzarella cheese substitute.

Store-cupboard satay

V Ve GF

No fancy sauces here – there's an instant satay saviour hiding in your kitchen and you didn't even know it. Double points for using up any leftover protein in your fridge.

1 tortilla (try a sweet chilli wrap or gluten-free alternative)
drizzle of sweet chilli sauce
a few ready-made crispy fried onions
handful of leftover cooked chicken, cooked prawns, marinated tofu pieces, or 1 hard-boiled egg
small handful of shredded crunchy lettuce leaves
a few slices of cucumber
spoon of crunchy peanut butter

Warm the tortilla according to the packet instructions, to make it nice and soft. Cut the tortilla from the edge nearest to you into the centre, then add the fillings as described below.

bottom left Drizzle over a generous amount of sweet chilli sauce, then scatter over a good layer of crispy onions to stick.

top left Add your protein, slicing up the egg or chicken as necessary.

top right Pile on some crunchy lettuce and cucumber slices.

bottom right Spread with the peanut butter.

Fold up the tortilla from the bottom left corner clockwise around the wrap. Eat straightaway.

> **WHY NOT TRY?**
> Pimping this up with a true Indonesian twist, using half sweet chilli and half kecap manis sauce.

Prawn cocktail

GF

What's better than sticking this retro classic in a soft wrap? Doubling up and sticking in some prawn cocktail crisps, too.

1 tortilla (try a seeded wrap or gluten-free alternative)
1 tablespoon tomato ketchup
1 tablespoon mayonnaise
½ lemon
freshly ground white pepper
small handful of cold, cooked peeled prawns
1–2 crunchy lettuce leaves, finely shredded
handful of prawn cocktail (or ready-salted) crisps
½ ripe avocado
salt

Cut the tortilla from the edge nearest to you into the centre, then assemble as follows.

bottom left Mix together the ketchup and mayo with a squeeze of lemon juice and season with some white pepper. Toss the prawns in the sauce and spoon onto the tortilla section.

top left Add the shredded lettuce.

top right Spread out the crisps over the section.

bottom right Use a fork to smash the avocado flesh over the base and squeeze over a little more lemon juice. Season with salt.

Fold up the tortilla from the bottom left corner clockwise around the wrap, squishing the crisp layer a little as you flip it over.

GOOD WITH the rest of the crisps on the side (well, why not!).

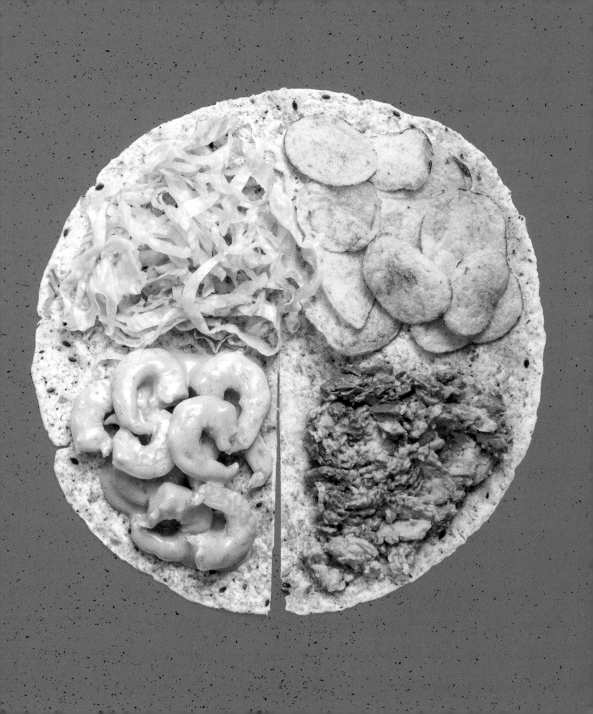

EASY CHEESY

Hot halloumi

Make halloumi the star in this simple but super-tasty toastie.

1 tortilla (try a white corn wrap or gluten-free alternative)
85–115g (3–4oz) halloumi
drizzle of olive or rapeseed oil
freshly ground black pepper
drizzle of runny honey, plus extra to serve
1 teaspoon harissa paste (use rose harissa if you can)
2 teaspoons soft butter

Cut the tortilla from the edge nearest to you into the centre. Cut the halloumi into 4–5 slices and heat a frying pan over a medium heat with a drizzle of oil. Grind a decent amount of black pepper over both sides of the cheese slices, pressing to stick, then fry for 1–2 minutes until golden on both sides. Assemble the tortilla as follows.

bottom left Drizzle a thick layer of honey all over.

top Arrange the halloumi slices over the top third with an extra grinding of pepper.

bottom right Spread the harissa paste and butter over the final section, mashing them together as you do.

Fold up the tortilla from the bottom left section clockwise around the wrap. Use a sandwich press to toast, or heat a frying pan, then add the wrap, harissa–butter side down, and fry for 1–2 minutes. Once the base is really crispy, flip the wrap and repeat for a minute or two until the other side is done too. Add another generous drizzle of honey and enjoy.

> **GOOD WITH** a leafy green salad and wedges of lemon.

Cheeseboard melt

Steer clear of feta and halloumi here, and go for melting favourites instead. Hard varieties like Cheddar, Stilton, Gruyère and Manchego are good, plus some softer types like Brie, Camembert, young goat and blue cheeses.

1 tortilla (try a seeded wrap or gluten-free alternative)
1 heaped tablespoon redcurrant jelly
1 heaped tablespoon diced red onion
115g (4oz) mixed cheeses
about 8 red grapes, halved lengthways

Cut the tortilla from the edge nearest to you into the centre, then add the fillings as follows.

bottom left Spread with the redcurrant jelly and top with the diced onion.

top left Add all of your soft cheeses. Cube those that can be and spread the rest.

top right Arrange the grapes cut-side down.

bottom right Grate the hard cheeses, toss to combine and press onto the final section.

Fold up the tortilla from the bottom left corner clockwise around the wrap. Use a sandwich press to toast, or heat in a hot frying pan for 2 minutes on each side until the outside is golden and the inside oozing.

> **WHY NOT TRY?**
> Freezing cheese. Cheese freezes surprisingly well, especially if you're going to cook with it anyway, so keep a container in the freezer, chuck in odds and ends and save them up for a monthly mega melt!

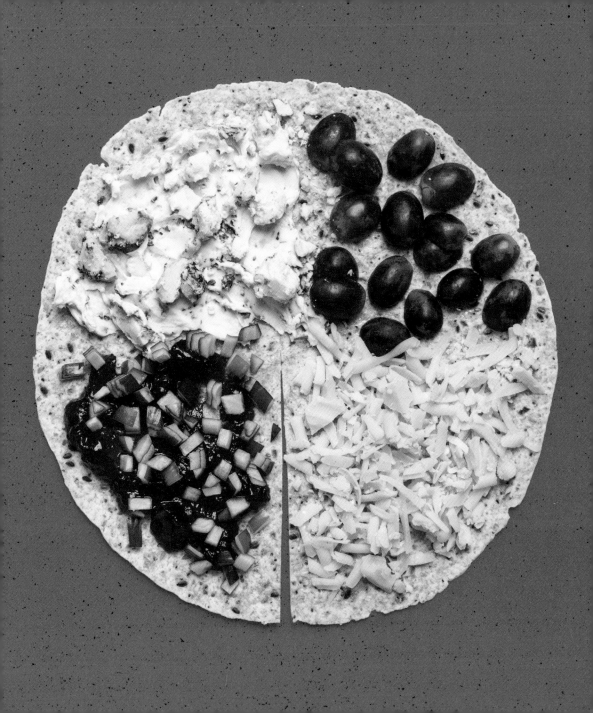

Garlic-buttered four cheese

(V) (GF)

This is quite simply utter filth, but on those occasions when only the cheesiest sandwich will satisfy, this is the one for you.

1 tortilla (try a large, soft white flour wrap or gluten-free alternative)
30g (1oz) soft butter
1–2 garlic cloves, finely grated or crushed
salt and freshly ground black pepper
small chunk of Gorgonzola
small chunk of Gruyère, grated
finger-length chunk of leek, very finely sliced
a few slices of mozzarella, or a small handful of ready-grated
small chunk of strong Cheddar, grated

Warm your tortilla according to the packet instructions. Mash the butter and garlic with some seasoning and spread over the whole tortilla, then cut from the edge nearest to you into the centre. Add toppings as follows.

bottom left Mash the Gorgonzola over the section.

top left Toss the grated Gruyère with half of the leek, and pat down to create a flat-ish layer.

top right Arrange the mozzarella slices.

bottom right Toss the grated Cheddar with the remaining leek, and pat down in the same way as the Gruyère.

Fold up the tortilla from the bottom left corner. Heat a large non-stick frying pan over a low–medium heat and cook the tortilla for 2–3 minutes on each side. If it's browning too much and the cheese hasn't completely melted, pop it in the microwave for 30 seconds on High or bake at 180°C/350°F to finish.

> **WHY NOT TRY?**
> Swapping in your favourite cheeses but keep the mozzarella for ooze!

Sweet & sour beetroot

(V) (GF)

This flavour combo would work nicely with plenty of other soft-ish cheeses if goat's cheese isn't your thing. Try crumbled feta, ricotta, or even a good buffalo mozzarella.

1 tortilla (try a wholewheat wrap or gluten-free alternative)
55g (2oz) soft goat's cheese
freshly ground black pepper
1 small–medium cooked beetroot, peeled if not
sea salt
1 tablespoon pomegranate molasses
1 teaspoon maple syrup
a few walnuts (toasted, if you like), roughly chopped
handful of lamb's lettuce (or other soft leaf)

Cut the tortilla from the edge nearest to you into the centre, then assemble as follows.

bottom left Spread generously with the cheese and season with pepper.

top left Slice the beetroot and arrange neatly over the section, seasoning with flaky sea salt.

top right Drizzle over the pomegranate molasses and maple syrup and scatter over the walnuts.

bottom right Pile on the leaves.

Fold up the tortilla from the bottom left corner clockwise around the wrap. Enjoy.

> **MAKE IT VEGAN**
> Swap the goat's cheese for cashew cheese.

Hot Saltimbocca sarnie

(GF)

If you're feeling fancy, using some garlic butter in place of the usual stuff would make this sandwich supreme.

1 tortilla (try a large,
    soft white flour wrap
    or gluten-free
    alternative)
2–3 knobs of butter
6–8 large sage leaves
good dollop of your
    favourite mustard
    – Dijon and grainy
    work well
2 slices of prosciutto
a few thick slices of
    mozzarella
handful of grated Gruyère

Cut the tortilla from the edge nearest to you into the centre. Add the butter and the sage leaves to a large frying pan, cook briefly to crisp up the sage. Lift the leaves from the pan with tongs so the herby butter stays in the pan. Assemble the tortilla as follows.

bottom left Spread with the mustard and ruffle the prosciutto slices on top.

top left and right Space out the mozzarella slices and scatter over the crispy sage leaves.

bottom right Pile on the grated Gruyère, patting it down to an even layer.

Fold up the tortilla from the bottom left section clockwise around the wrap. Carefully lift it back into the pan and fry until golden and crispy on both sides – you might want to add more butter when you turn the toastie over. Make sure the cheese is molten – if not, turn the heat down, cover the pan and leave for a few more minutes.

> **WHY NOT TRY?**
> Swapping the prosciutto for any thinly sliced smoked or cured ham.

Chic-Greek toastie

Double cheese? You heard it here first. Covering the right half of your tortilla entirely with cheese means it wraps around all of your other fillings. Why settle for one layer of melting cheese when you can have two?

1 tortilla (try a wholewheat wrap or gluten-free alternative)
½ small courgette, trimmed, halved and sliced
drizzle of extra virgin olive oil
salt and freshly ground black pepper
a few pinches dried oregano
1–2 plum tomatoes, sliced
a few stoned Kalamata olives, roughly chopped
splash of red wine vinegar
85g (3oz) feta, light or full-fat
small handful of ready-grated mozzarella

Cut the tortilla from the edge nearest to you into the centre, then add the fillings as follows.

bottom left Toss the courgette slices with a drizzle of oil, salt, pepper and the dried oregano. Spread the slices evenly over the section.

top left Layer on the tomato slices and olives, then sprinkle over the smallest splash of vinegar to season them.

top and bottom right Finely crumble the feta and toss with the mozzarella. Fill the whole right half of the tortilla, leaving a little gap at 3 o'clock for folding.

Fold up the tortilla from the bottom left corner clockwise around the wrap; the cheese will wrap around all of the veg. Use a sandwich press to toast, or heat in a hot frying pan for 1–2 minutes on each side until the tortilla is golden and crisp and the mozzarella has melted.

> **GOOD WITH** a quick red onion salad. Roast red onion wedges until soft, then dress with olive oil, pomegranate molasses and honey.

Veggie tricolour

A play on the classic Italian salad, but creamy ricotta replaces the mozzarella. If you have any basil leaves you can add these too.

1 tortilla (try a regular, soft white flour wrap or gluten-free alternative)
3–4 tablespoons of ricotta
freshly ground black pepper
small handful of mint leaves
the nicest red tomato you can find, thickly sliced
salt
2 tablespoons basil pesto

Warm the tortilla according to the packet instructions. Cut the tortilla from the edge nearest to you into the centre, then follow the order of toppings below.

bottom left Spread thickly with ricotta and season with pepper.

top left Arrange the mint leaves like a jigsaw puzzle in a single layer.

top right Add the tomato slices, seasoning well with salt.

bottom right Spread with the pesto.

Fold up the tortilla from the bottom left corner clockwise around the wrap.

> **WHY NOT TRY?**
> Adding a sprinkle of toasted pine nuts to the ricotta layer.

KFC (Korean fried cheese)

(V) (GF)

If you want to bulk up the greens in this one, add some finely shredded cabbage, kale or spring greens along with the spring onions.

1 tortilla (try a sweet chilli wrap or gluten-free alternative)
a few spoons of kimchi
1 spring onion, thinly sliced
small handful of grated Cheddar
small handful of grated Gruyère
salt and freshly ground black pepper

Prepare the tortilla by cutting from the edge nearest to you into the centre. Top the tortilla as follows.

bottom left Roughly chop the kimchi, then spread over and scatter with the spring onion.

top Add the grated Cheddar.

bottom right Finish with the grated Gruyère.

Season the topped tortilla, then fold up the tortilla from the bottom left section clockwise around the wrap. Use a sandwich press to toast, or cook in a hot frying pan for 2 minutes on each side until the cheese is molten.

GOOD WITH all your favourite condiments: crispy chilli oil, Indonesian sweet soy sauce, Sriracha or Japanese mayo.

Cheeseburger toastie

Change your burger game forever. Ditching the bun for our stacked tortilla version means no more spills (just flavour thrills . . .)

1 tortilla (try a large brioche-style wrap or gluten-free alternative)
1–2 tablespoons burger sauce or mayonnaise
small wedge of white onion or 1 shallot, thinly sliced
a few slices of gherkin
1 beef or bean burger patty, cooked following packet instructions
dollop of tomato ketchup or burger relish
2–3 slices of Monterey Jack or other burger cheese
¼ teaspoon sesame seeds

Warm your tortilla according to the packet instructions to make it lovely and soft. Add the fillings as follows.

bottom left Spread with some burger sauce or mayo.

top left Scatter over the onion and gherkin slices.

top right Add the burger patty and top with a dollop of ketchup or relish.

bottom right Overlap the cheese slices to cover the section and sprinkle with the sesame seeds.

Fold up the tortilla from the bottom left corner clockwise around the wrap. Use a sandwich press to toast, or cook in a hot frying pan for 1–2 minutes on each side until the cheese has melted and the tortilla is golden.

> **WHY NOT TRY?**
> Making a meal of it by eating with a pile of curly or straight fries.

Mexican chipotle chicken melt

If you've any leftover rice or beans, add these with the sweetcorn and elevate this toastie to a full-scale burrito.

1 tortilla (try a wholewheat wrap or gluten-free alternative)

small dollop of soured cream, Greek yogurt or mayonnaise

2–3 tablespoons of sweetcorn, tinned or frozen

handful of coriander, baby kale or spinach

2 tablespoons barbecue sauce

½–1 teaspoon chipotle paste (depending how hot you can handle it!)

1 cooked chicken thigh (or equivalent amount of cooked chicken)

2–3 slices of Swiss cheese, such as Emmental

Prepare the tortilla by cutting from the edge nearest to you into the centre. Top the tortilla as follows.

bottom left Spread over the soured cream, yogurt or mayo. Scatter over the corn with any greens you choose to use.

top Mix together the barbecue sauce and chipotle paste, then finely shred the chicken meat using two forks. Stir the sauce through the chicken and pile onto the wrap.

bottom right Add the cheese slices.

Fold up the tortilla from the bottom left section clockwise around the wrap. Use a sandwich press to toast, or heat in a hot frying pan for 2 minutes on each side until golden. Eat straightaway.

EAT WITH a big bowl of guacamole. Also good with the quick pickled onions from the Bombay Bhaji Sandwich (see page 109).

LOVE YOUR
LEFTOVERS

LEFTOVER ROAST DINNER:
All-day roast

Everybody knows the best bit about a roast dinner is piling all the leftovers into a sandwich the following day . . .

1 tortilla (try a large, soft white flour wrap)
1 heaped tablespoon caramelised onion chutney
a spoon of leftover stuffing, or 2 roast parsnips, thinly sliced
1 heaped tablespoon mayonnaise
2–3 slices of leftover roast chicken
large handful of salad leaves
1 heaped tablespoon cranberry sauce
1–2 slices of ham

Warm the tortilla according to the packet instructions, then lay on a chopping board and make a cut from the edge nearest to you into the centre. Add the fillings as follows.

bottom left Spread over the chutney, then top with crumbled stuffing or sliced parsnips.

top left Spread with mayonnaise and top with the chicken.

top right Add the salad leaves.

bottom right Spread with the cranberry sauce and top with the ham.

Carefully fold up the tortilla from the bottom left corner clockwise around the wrap. Enjoy.

> **MAKE IT VEGGIE**
> Swap the chicken for leftover nut roast and the ham for slices of cheese – Brie or Camembert pairs nicely with the chutney.

LEFTOVER SAUSAGES:

Best-ever sausage sarnie

If pickled red cabbage isn't your thing, braised red cabbage, sauerkraut or even a little finely sliced raw cabbage would make a good alternative.

1 tortilla (try a seeded wrap)
2 tablespoons caramelised onion chutney
spoonful of pickled red cabbage
1–2 leftover sausages (pork or veggie), halved lengthways
2 teaspoons grainy mustard
a few slices of extra mature Cheddar

Warm the tortilla according to the packet instructions, so it's soft enough to wrap around the fillings without breaking. Cut the tortilla from the edge nearest you into the centre, then fill as follows.

bottom left Spread generously with the chutney.

top left Drain the juices from the cabbage, then add to this section.

top right Add the sausage slices and mustard.

bottom right Add the cheese.

Carefully fold up the tortilla from the bottom left corner clockwise around the wrap. Use a sandwich press to toast, or cook in a hot frying pan for 2 minutes on each side until the cheese is melted and the tortilla is super crispy.

> **MAKE IT VEGAN**
> Use your favourite Cheddar substitute with vegan sausages.

LEFTOVER DAAL:

Chilli-cheese & daal

(Ve) (GF)

Daal is a protein-packed, frugal supper that's gained in popularity over recent years. Just don't be tempted to reheat it first – it spreads much better from cold.

1 tortilla (try a sweet potato wrap or gluten-free alternative)
2 heaped tablespoons mango chutney
small handful of spinach leaves
1 tablespoon natural or coconut yogurt
salt and freshly ground black pepper
big spoonful of leftover cold daal
small handful of grated Cheddar, or Cheddar substitute
few sprigs of coriander
few slices of fresh red chilli

Cut the tortilla from the edge nearest to you into the centre, then add the fillings as follows.

bottom left Spread with the chutney.

top left Toss the spinach leaves with the yogurt to coat. Pile onto this section of tortilla and season.

top right Pile on the daal.

bottom right Toss the cheese with leaves picked from the coriander and as much chilli as you can handle. Pile onto the section then pat down.

Fold up the tortilla from the bottom left corner clockwise around the wrap, and press down with your hand. Use a sandwich press to toast, or cook in a hot frying pan for 1–2 minutes on each side until the tortilla is golden and the daal is warm.

> **WHY NOT TRY?**
> No daal? Any leftover curry would be good in this tortilla.

LEFTOVER ROAST BEEF:

Roast beef Reuben

GF

Russian dressing is authentic, but you should already have the means to knock up a cheat's version in your store-cupboard.

1 tortilla (try a seeded wrap or gluten-free alternative)
4 teaspoons mayonnaise
1 tablespoon tomato ketchup
good splash of Worcestershire sauce
big spoonful sauerkraut
2–3 thin slices of leftover beef or steak
a few slices of Swiss cheese, such as Emmental

Warm the tortilla according to the packet instructions, then transfer to a chopping board and cut into the centre from the edge nearest to you. Add the toppings in the following order.

bottom left Mix the mayo, ketchup and Worcestershire sauce together then spread over the section.

top left Make an even layer of the sauerkraut.

top right Top with the thinly sliced beef.

bottom right Add the cheese.

Fold up the tortilla from the bottom left corner clockwise around the wrap. Eat with pickles or fries.

WHY NOT TRY?
Shop-bought pastrami when there's no leftovers.

LEFTOVER VEG:
Veggie bahn-miso

Ve GF

As long as your veg can be eaten raw, it can be used up in this feisty lunch offering.

leftover veg, such as carrots, cabbage, peppers, radishes, cucumber, swede, spring onions, celeriac, sugar snaps
1 tablespoon rice wine vinegar
1 teaspoon caster sugar
1 tortilla (try a sweet chilli wrap or gluten-free alternative)
drizzle of sweet or hot chilli sauce
½ handful of roasted peanuts or cashews, roughly chopped
fresh herbs, such as mint leaves or coriander, or a mixture
1 teaspoon white miso
3 tablespoons hummus

Finely shred the veg. Mix the vinegar and sugar together until the sugar has dissolved, then toss through the veg. Leave to marinate while you prepare everything else.

Warm the tortilla according to the packet instructions, then transfer to a chopping board and cut into the centre from the edge nearest to you. Assemble as follows.

bottom left Drizzle generously with the chilli sauce.

top left Pile on the quick pickled veg, shaking off any excess marinade.

top right Scatter with the nuts and herbs.

bottom right Mash the miso into the hummus, then spread over.

Fold up the tortilla from the bottom left corner clockwise around the wrap, then tuck in.

> **WHY NOT TRY?**
> Swapping the chilli sauce for hoisin, plum or satay sauce.

LEFTOVER ROAST POTATOES:

Potato pizza bread

(V) (GF)

If you're a fan of pizza bianco, those classic, Italian white-topped pizzas, then you'll love this (and there's no shame in cooking extra roasties just so you can justify making one).

1 tortilla (try a wholewheat wrap or gluten-free alternative)
4 tablespoons crème fraîche
2 heaped tablespoons ready-made crispy fried onions
salt and freshly ground black pepper
30–55g (1–2oz) grated Emmental or Gruyère
a few pinches of dried rosemary
2 leftover roast potatoes, diced

Cut your tortilla from the edge nearest to you into the centre, then assemble as follows.

bottom left Spread over the crème fraîche, scatter with the onions and season with salt and plenty of pepper.

top Scatter evenly with the cheese followed by the rosemary.

bottom right Add the roast potatoes.

Fold up the tortilla from the bottom left section clockwise around the wrap, and use a sandwich press to toast, or cook in a hot frying pan for 1–3 minutes on each side until golden and crisp.

> **WHY NOT TRY?**
> Using fresh rosemary from your garden or balcony. Pick a few needles, finely chop and use in place of the dried.

LEFTOVER BOLOGNESE SAUCE:
Sloppy Joe toastie

(V) (GF)

The great American classic uses a sauce made from scratch, but leftover ragù from spaghetti Bolognese makes a fine substitute.

1 tortilla (try a regular, soft white flour wrap or gluten-free alternative)
I heaped tablespoon tomato ketchup
a few very thin onion slices
a few gherkin or pickle slices
leftover beef or lentil Bolognese sauce
a few slices of mild, hard cheese, such as Cheddar or Swiss

Cut your tortilla from the edge nearest to you into the centre, then assemble as follows.

bottom left Spread with the ketchup.

top left Scatter over a thin layer of onion and pickle slices.

top right Spread with a thick layer of Bolognese sauce.

bottom right Add the cheese.

Fold up the tortilla from the bottom left corner clockwise around the wrap, and use a sandwich press to toast, or cook in a hot frying pan for 2 minutes on each side until the cheese is melted.

> **GOOD WITH** coleslaw and crisps.

LEFTOVER MASH:

Spinach, feta & potato gözleme

(V) (GF)

Gözleme are Turkish stuffed flatbreads filled with all sorts of savoury deliciousness, but potato, spinach and some sort of cheese usually feature heavily.

1 tortilla (try a regular,
   soft white flour wrap
   or gluten-free
   alternative)
large dollop of leftover
   mash
1 spring onion, thinly sliced
handful of spinach leaves
salt and freshly ground
   black pepper
85–115g (3–4oz) feta
zest of ½ lemon
olive oil

Prepare the tortilla by making a cut from the edge nearest to you into the centre, then assemble as follows.

bottom left Spread over the mash and scatter with the spring onion.

top Add the spinach with a little seasoning.

bottom right Crumble the feta and mix with the lemon zest and some black pepper before scattering over the final section.

Fold up the tortilla from the bottom left section clockwise around the wrap. Add a splash of olive oil to a frying pan, and cook for 1–2 minutes on each side until really golden and crisp.

> **WHY NOT TRY?**
> Adding chorizo, kabanos or another spicy sausage.

LEFTOVER COOKED VEG:
Moroccan veg & chickpea

Ve GF

This works just as nicely with earthy roasted roots like carrot, parsnip and beetroot, as it does with Mediterranean veg like aubergine, peppers and courgettes.

1 tortilla (try a seeded wrap or gluten-free alternative)

drizzle of pomegranate molasses

handful of leftover cooked vegetables, roughly chopped up

2 tablespoons tahini

3–4 tablespoons cooked chickpeas

handful of soft salad leaves

Warm the tortilla according to the packet instructions, then transfer to a chopping board and cut into the centre from the edge nearest to you. Assemble as follows.

bottom left Drizzle over the sticky pomegranate molasses.

top left Pile on all the leftover veg.

top right Spread over the tahini – loosen it with a splash of water if you're finding it too thick. Scatter over the chickpeas.

bottom right Add the salad leaves.

Fold up the tortilla from the bottom left corner clockwise around the wrap.

WHY NOT TRY?
Using leftover pulses like cooked beans or lentils instead of the chickpeas.

DELICIOUSLY DIFFERENT

Lazy lasagne

Home-made lasagne is a real labour of love. This clever hack gives you all of that feel-good flavour, but with none of the fuss.

splash of olive oil

55g (2oz) minced beef, quorn mince or sausage meat (gluten-free, if needed)

1 tortilla (try a large, soft white flour wrap or gluten-free alternative)

2–3 tablespoons tomato pasta sauce

a few slices of mozzarella, or a small handful ready-grated

a few basil leaves

55g (2oz) ricotta

small chunk of Parmesan (or a vegetarian alternative)

salt and freshly ground black pepper

Heat the oil in a non-stick frying pan and cook the mince or sausage meat for a few minutes, stirring, until browned and cooked through. Lay the wrap on a chopping board and make a cut from the edge nearest to you into the centre. Assemble as follows.

bottom left Spread with tomato pasta sauce. Add the cooked meat or mince.

top Add the mozzarella and top with the basil leaves.

bottom right Spoon on the ricotta then use the back of the spoon to spread it out a little. Add a really good grating of Parmesan over the top.

Season the whole topped tortilla with salt and pepper, then begin to fold up from the bottom left section clockwise around the wrap. Gently cook in a frying pan for 2 minutes on each side until really crispy – don't worry if some of the filling escapes, this one is meant to be a bit messy.

> **GOOD WITH** a leafy salad tossed with a balsamic dressing.

Green goddess

Keep it seasonal by swapping the courgette for baby kale during the winter.

1 tortilla (try a wholewheat or beetroot wrap or gluten-free alternative)

a good dollop of green olive tapenade (check it's vegan)

a few marinated artichoke hearts, pulled into pieces

1 baby courgette, grated

two good dollops of hummus

Warm the tortilla following the packet instructions, then cut from the side nearest you into the middle. Follow the order of toppings below.

bottom left Spread over a thin layer of the tapenade.

top left Arrange the artichoke pieces.

top right Add the grated courgette.

bottom right Spread the hummus more thickly than the tapenade.

Fold up the tortilla from the bottom left corner clockwise around the wrap. Enjoy warm or cold.

WHY NOT TRY?
Basil pesto instead of the tapenade.

Bombay bhaji sandwich

If you can't get to Mumbai to try one of their famous grilled vegetable and cheese sandwiches on Chowpatty Beach, eating this bhaji-stuffed number on your sofa is the next best thing.

1 small red onion,
   thinly sliced
2 tablespoons red
   wine vinegar
1 tablespoon caster sugar
1 tortilla (try a wholewheat
   wrap)
1 heaped tablespoon
   of Greek yogurt or
   coconut yogurt
2–3 cooked onion bhajis
   (use vegan if needed,
   broken into chunks)
1 tablespoon mint sauce,
   from a jar
small chunk of cucumber,
   thinly sliced

Combine the onions, vinegar and sugar, and microwave for 30 seconds on High, or heat together in a small saucepan until the liquid is hand-hot. Set aside to pickle.

Warm the tortilla according to the packet instructions, then make a cut from the edge nearest to you into the centre. Assemble as follows.

bottom left Spread with the yogurt, then lift some of the onions from their pickling liquid and scatter over.

top Add the chunks of onion bhaji.

bottom right Spread with the mint sauce then top with cucumber slices.

Fold up the tortilla from the bottom left section clockwise around the wrap. Eat quickly if you don't want a soggy bottom, with extra pickled onions on the side.

WHY NOT TRY?
Swapping the cucumber and mint sauce elements for any salad and your favourite Indian accompaniments.

Marinated courgette, herb & soft cheese

These dressed courgettes are so tasty we suggest you make a double batch and thank us later.

2 teaspoons extra virgin olive oil
zest of ½ lemon plus 2 teaspoons juice
a large pinch of English mustard powder
salt and freshly ground black pepper
1 small courgette (cut lengthways), trimmed
1 tortilla (try a seeded wrap or gluten-free alternative)
some garlic and herb soft cheese
small handful of black olives, stoned
small handful of basil leaves

In a medium mixing bowl, add the oil, lemon zest and juice, the mustard powder and some seasoning. Mix together well, then cut the courgette into ribbons using a swivel peeler. Toss through the dressing and leave to marinate for at least 5 minutes – but the longer, the tastier.

Warm the tortilla according to the packet instructions, then make a cut from the edge nearest to you into the centre of the tortilla and add the fillings as follows.

bottom left Spread with a good layer of herby cheese. Crush the olives using the bottom of the olive jar and scatter over the cheese.

top left and right Pile on the courgette ribbons, drizzling over any dressing left in the bowl.

bottom right Tear over some basil leaves.

Fold up the tortilla from the bottom left section clockwise around the wrap, and enjoy.

> **MAKE IT VEGAN**
> Use a dairy-free garlic and herb cheese spread.

Spiced lamb pide

(GF)

Pide is a favourite street food in Turkey – it's a bit like a pizza, basically. We've taken one of the classic toppings and stuffed it into a tortilla instead, so it's even easier to eat when you're on the go.

55–85g (2–3oz) minced lamb
1 teaspoon each garlic granules and ground cumin
2–3 tablespoons tomato purée
freshly ground black pepper
1 tortilla (try a large corn and wheat wrap or gluten-free alternative)
¼ white onion, very thinly sliced (on a mandoline if you have one)
½ green or red pepper (or a mixture), sliced
handful of grated medium or mature Cheddar
1 heaped tablespoon finely chopped parsley

Fry the mince in a non-stick frying pan until starting to brown. Stir in the garlic granules and cumin and cook for a further 1–2 minutes.

Spread tomato purée all over the tortilla, then cut into the centre of the wrap from the edge nearest to you. Add the fillings as follows.

bottom left Spoon over the cooked lamb.

top Scatter over the onions and peppers.

bottom right Add the cheese.

Scatter the parsley over the topped tortilla, then fold up the tortilla from the bottom left section clockwise around the wrap. Use a sandwich press to toast, or cook in a hot frying pan for 1–2 minutes on each side until golden.

> **MAKE IT VEGGIE**
> Instead of the minced lamb, finely some mushrooms, and fry until all the liquid has evaporated and the mushrooms are browning before adding the spices.

Crispy halloumi, kale & beetroot

Did you know that you can crisp up halloumi in your sandwich press? No oil, 2–3 minutes with the lid down, and hey presto – halloumi hack!

3 slices of halloumi
splash of olive or
    rapeseed oil
1 tortilla (try a sweet
    potato wrap or
    gluten-free alternative)
½ ripe avocado, flesh
    mashed with a squeeze
    of lemon or lime to
    prevent browning
sprinkle of pumpkin seeds,
    toasted if you like
2–3 tablespoons of
    beetroot hummus
drizzle of sesame oil
small handful of chopped
    kale (or 1 whole leaf),
    thick stalks discarded

Cook the halloumi slices in a frying pan with a splash of oil for a few minutes, until golden and crisp on the outside. Meanwhile, warm the tortilla according to the packet instructions, then make a cut from the edge nearest to you into the centre of the wrap. Follow the order of toppings below.

bottom left Spread with the mashed avocado, then scatter with the seeds.

top left Add the hot halloumi slices.

top right Spoon over the beetroot hummus.

bottom right In a bowl, drizzle a little sesame oil all over the kale leaves, then scrunch the leaves heavily so they become evenly coated and slightly softer. Add to the final section of the wrap.

Fold up the tortilla from the bottom left corner clockwise around the wrap. Eat.

> **GOOD WITH** a pile of sweet potato or parsnip crisps.

Red pepper gyros

Any dish that wraps chips inside bread is a winner in our book. We've stayed true to the original, simply swapping in a tortilla for the traditional pita and using roasted peppers as the star – but leftover roast lamb or chicken would work nicely, too.

1 tortilla (try a large, soft white flour wrap or gluten-free alternative)
30g (1oz) thick Greek yogurt
1 tablespoon tahini
1 garlic clove, finely grated or crushed
salt and freshly ground black pepper
small handful of frozen fries, cooked following the packet instructions
55g (2oz) feta, crumbled
1 whole roasted pepper from a jar, patted dry using kitchen towel
lemon wedge, to serve

Warm the tortilla following the packet instructions, then make a cut into the centre from the edge nearest to you. Assemble as follows.

bottom left Mix the yogurt, tahini, garlic and 2 teaspoons of water with seasoning to make a sauce. Spread over.

top left Pile on the hot fries.

top right Add the crumbled feta.

bottom right Roughly chop the pepper and layer up in the final section.

Season with a squeeze of lemon, then fold up the tortilla from the bottom left corner clockwise around the wrap. Eat immediately before the fries get soggy.

> **MAKE IT VEGAN**
> Ditch the yogurt and mix the tahini with 1 tablespoon of water, the garlic and seasoning. In place of the feta, roughly chop a plum tomato, a few black olives, capers and red onion and mix to create a salty salsa.

Buffalo chicken salad

A healthier take on the classic, but still with that all-important sweet–spicy combo.

1 tortilla (try a white corn wrap or gluten-free alternative)

a little American hot sauce, such as Frank's

a little runny honey

a few slices of cooked chicken

small chunk of iceberg lettuce, finely shredded

a good squirt of mayonnaise

chunk of hard blue cheese, such as Stilton

Warm the tortilla according to the packet instructions, then make a cut into the centre of the tortilla from the edge nearest to you. Top the tortilla as follows.

bottom left Drizzle over equal quantities of hot sauce and honey.

top left Make an even layer of the chicken pieces.

top right Pile on the shredded lettuce.

bottom right Spread first with the mayo, then crumble over the cheese.

Fold up the tortilla from the bottom left corner clockwise around the wrap.

> **WHY NOT TRY?**
> Using hot crumbed chicken strips.

Spanish blue

A creamy blue cheese pairs wonderfully with the crispness of the leaves and pear, but to keep it truly Spanish lots of thin slices of Manchego cheese would work brilliantly, too.

1 tortilla (try a regular, soft white flour wrap or gluten-free alternative)

1 heaped tablespoon membrillo or quince paste (or a plum chutney or similar)

55g (2oz) of your favourite soft, spreadable blue cheese

2–3 red radicchio leaves

1 small (or ½ large) unripe pear, cored and thinly sliced

Cut the tortilla from the edge nearest to you into the centre. Add the fillings as follows.

bottom left Spread over the membrillo or quince paste.

top left Spread over the blue cheese.

top right Arrange the radicchio leaves.

bottom right Arrange the crisp pear slices.

Fold up the tortilla from the bottom left corner clockwise around the wrap, and eat immediately or pack into a lunchbox for later.

WHY NOT TRY?
Toasting the wrap for a few minutes in a sandwich press. Just swap the position of the pear and cheese layers – radicchio is delicious cooked, and is one of the few leafy elements that benefits from being on the 'outside' of your toastie.

SWEET TREATS

Rocky road s'mores

One classic gets mashed up with another. Quite literally with this, as the chocolate and marshmallow melt into the tortilla, sticking the whole stack together . . . yummm. Use a mini tortilla for the perfect snack for one.

1 mini tortilla (try a mini white flour wrap)
a little chocolate spread
1 brazil nut (or hazelnuts, peanuts or macadamias) roughly chopped
1 small, crunchy biscuit, such as Biscoff or Petit Beurre
1 square of dark chocolate
1 regular marshmallow

Prepare your mini tortilla by cutting from the edge nearest to you into the centre. Assemble as follows.

bottom left Spread with chocolate spread and scatter over the chopped nuts.

top left Add the biscuit.

top right Add the square of chocolate.

bottom right Squish on the marshmallow or snip in half with scissors.

Fold up the tortilla from the bottom left corner clockwise around the wrap. Use a sandwich press to toast, or cook in a hot frying pan for 30 seconds to 1 minute on each side until the chocolate and marshmallows are just melted – too long and you risk too much leakage, so take care. Leave for a minute or two to firm up and cool slightly before eating.

> **MAKE IT VEGGIE**
> Use vegetarian marshmallows.

Perfect PBJ

Ve **GF**

When you suddenly crave something sweet, this recipe is ideal. It's made in minutes, using only a handful of ingredients – and most will be in your kitchen cupboards already.

1 tortilla (try a wholewheat wrap or gluten-free alternative)
3–4 strawberries, sliced
a big spoonful of peanut butter
a big spoonful of berry jam (of your choice)
small handful of roasted peanuts (or almonds), roughly chopped
dusting of icing sugar

Cut the tortilla from the edge nearest to you into the centre, and add the fillings as follows.

bottom left Add the strawberry slices neatly, leaving as few gaps as possible.

top Spread over the peanut butter.

bottom right Spread over the jam and sprinkle on the nuts.

Carefully fold up the tortilla from the bottom left section clockwise around the wrap, then toast using a sandwich press or cook in a hot frying pan for 1–2 minutes on each side. Dust with icing sugar.

WHY NOT TRY?
Adding a layer of sweetened cream cheese under the strawberry slices for a PBJ cheesecake.

Club tropicana

Just as good for breakfast or brunch as it is for a pudding. You could even add a little extra crunch with a sprinkle of granola.

1 tortilla (try a seeded
    wrap or gluten-free
    alternative)
dusting of icing sugar
a big spoonful of coconut
    yogurt
a few ripe slices of mango
zest of 1 lime plus a
    squeeze of juice
2 tablespoons toasted
    desiccated coconut
1 teaspoon demerara sugar

Dust one side of the tortilla with a little icing sugar and rub in. Heat a frying pan, add the tortilla and lightly toast on both sides – don't worry if it puffs up, just squash it back down with a fish slice. Slide onto a chopping board, sugared side-up, and let it firm up for a minute – it should look shiny and pale golden. Cut into the tortilla from the edge nearest to you until you reach the centre. Add the fillings as follows.

bottom left Spread with a thick layer of coconut yogurt.

top Arrange the mango slices.

bottom right Mix together the lime zest, coconut and demerara sugar. Sprinkle over the final section of tortilla, then squeeze over some lime juice.

Fold up the tortilla from the bottom left section clockwise around the wrap. Enjoy with a pile of napkins.

WHY NOT TRY?
Swapping the mango for other tropical fruits.

Sticky toffee pudding

Malt loaf has all the richness of a traditional sticky toffee pudding but none of the faff.

1 tortilla (try a regular, soft white flour wrap)

1–2 tablespoons thick toffee or caramel sauce, plus extra to serve

5 large, soft dates (like Medjool), stoned

2 slices of malt loaf

2 knobs of soft butter

Cut the tortilla from the edge nearest to you into the centre. Add the fillings as described.

bottom left Spread over the toffee or caramel sauce.

top left Dice the dates and dot over.

top right Squash on the slices of malt loaf – you might need to overlap a bit to fit.

bottom right Spread thickly with butter.

Fold up the tortilla from the bottom left corner clockwise around the wrap, firmly pressing down with your hand between each fold to stick the fillings in place and squash everything a little flatter. Cook in a hot frying pan for 2 minutes on each side until the tortilla is golden and crisp. Enjoy with extra toffee or caramel sauce on the side.

GOOD WITH a scoop of vanilla ice cream or some cold cream for dunking.

Spiced apple pie

Home-made apple pie, just like Mum used to make . . . but easier, and quicker, and the perfect portion for one.

1 tortilla (try a wholewheat wrap or gluten-free alternative)

3 tablespoons smooth or chunky apple sauce from a jar

½ small eating apple, thinly sliced

1 tablespoon very soft butter or dairy-free (vegan) spread

¼ teaspoon mixed spice, ground cinnamon or pumpkin pie spice

1½ teaspoons caster sugar

Cut the tortilla from the edge nearest to you into the centre, and top in the following order.

bottom left Spread over the apple sauce.

top Scatter with the chopped apple.

bottom right Mash together the butter or spread, your chosen spice and the sugar. Spread half all over the final section of the tortilla.

Fold up the tortilla from the bottom left section clockwise around the wrap. Smear the rest of the spiced butter all over the outside of the tortilla – using your fingers might be easiest. Toast in a sandwich press, or heat a frying pan and cook the tortilla in the hot pan for 1 minute on each side until golden.

> **GOOD WITH** whipped cream, whipped coconut cream or vanilla ice cream. And lots of maple or golden syrup.

Salted caramel banana bread

(V)

TikTok's favourite hack meets TikTok's favourite recipe.

1 tortilla (try a brioche-
 style wrap)
a little Biscoff biscuit
 spread
1 slice of Madeira loaf cake
 (or other plain sponge)
1 small banana, sliced
a little caramel spread/
 sauce from a jar
sea salt flakes
knob of butter

Warm the tortilla according to the packet instructions to make it a little more flexible, then make a cut from the edge nearest to you into the centre. Top the tortilla in the following order.

bottom left Spread with the biscuit spread.

top left Crumble over chunks of the cake slice.

top right Arrange the banana slices.

bottom right Spread with the caramel sauce and top with a pinch of sea salt flakes. Don't be too generous with the caramel or it'll ooze out and burn while toasting.

Fold up the tortilla from the bottom left corner clockwise around the wrap. Melt the butter in a hot frying pan and cook the tortilla for 1–2 minutes on each side until crisp.

> **MAKE IT VEGAN**
> Use a vegan sponge cake plus dairy-free caramel sauce. Biscoff spread is vegan.

Churro tacos

(V) (GF)

Heavy with cinnamon and sugar, a big pile of these would make a great sweet alternative to nachos if you're feeding a crowd. Just use smaller wraps instead – these topping quantities will be enough for two mini tortillas.

1 tortilla (try a regular, soft white flour wrap or gluten-free alternative)

30g (1oz) very soft salted butter

1 teaspoon ground cinnamon

2 tablespoons golden caster (or light brown) sugar

warm chocolate dipping sauce, to serve

Cut the tortilla from the edge nearest to you into the centre. Mash together the butter and cinnamon and assemble as follows.

bottom left to bottom right Spread the whole tortilla with the cinnamon-butter – it makes a generous amount, so you might not need it all. Sprinkle with 1 tablespoon of sugar.

Fold up the tortilla from the bottom left corner clockwise around the wrap. Heat a small frying pan over a high heat, then add the tortilla and fry for just 1 minute on each side until golden brown. Some of the cinnamon butter will ooze out, so use a spoon to baste the tortilla with this as it cooks. If the cinnamon starts smoking, turn down the heat.

Lift the tortilla straight onto a plate sprinkled with the second tablespoon of sugar and flip it a few times to generously coat. Let it crisp up for a minute, then enjoy with the chocolate dipping sauce.

GOOD WITH warm raspberry jam instead of the classic chocolate sauce.

Blueberry cheesecake

Any berries would work nicely in this clever twist, as would any other curds, such as lime or passionfruit.

1 tortilla (try a brioche-style wrap or gluten-free alternative)
2 tablespoons icing sugar, plus extra for dusting
a spoonful of lemon curd
handful of blueberries, halved if large
85g (3oz) cream cheese
¼ teaspoon vanilla extract or paste

Dust one side of the tortilla with icing sugar and warm in a frying pan briefly on both sides. Slide onto baking parchment, sugared side-up, (it'll be a little sticky) and cut into the tortilla from the edge nearest to you until you reach the centre. Assemble as follows.

bottom left Spread with the lemon curd.

top left Arrange the blueberries.

top right + bottom right Mash together the 2 tablespoons of icing sugar, cream cheese and vanilla. Spread over the right half of the tortilla, leaving a gap for folding at 3 o'clock.

Carefully fold up the tortilla from the bottom left corner clockwise around the wrap, and dust with more icing sugar before eating.

GOOD WITH extra berries served on the side.

Chocolate truffle

You could get really indulgent with this and add some candied or honey-roasted nuts instead of plain, plus white chocolate spread instead of milk or dark. Whatever tickles your tastebuds!

1 tortilla (try a wholewheat wrap or gluten-free alternative)

1–2 tablespoons of chocolate-hazelnut spread

3 tablespoons whole hazelnuts, chopped (or 2 tablespoons ready-chopped)

1 tablespoon icing sugar

1–2 tablespoons of cream cheese

Warm the tortilla according to the packet instructions, then make a cut from the edge nearest to you into the centre. Follow the order of toppings below.

bottom left Spread with a thick layer of chocolate spread.

top left Sprinkle over the nuts.

top right Sprinkle over the icing sugar.

bottom right Spread a layer of cream cheese to the same thickness as the chocolate spread layer.

Carefully fold up the tortilla from the bottom left corner clockwise around the wrap. Let it sit for a few minutes to allow the flavours to absorb and soften the wrap, then eat.

MAKE IT VEGAN
Use a vegan cream cheese substitute and dairy-free chocolate spread.

INDEX

All vegetarian or vegan recipes are in **bold**.

J

jam
> **Perfect PBJ** 126

K

kale
> **Crispy halloumi, kale & beetroot** 114
> Mexican chipotle chicken melt 80
KFC (Korean fried cheese) 76
kimchi
> **KFC (Korean fried cheese)** 76

L

lamb
> Spiced lamb pide 113
Lazy lasagne 105
leek
> **Garlic-buttered four cheese** 67
lemon curd
> **Blueberry cheesecake** 138
lettuce, *see also* salad leaves
> Brilliant BLT 34
> Buffalo chicken salad 118
> Fish finger foldie 49
> Ham & sweet pea 42
> Prawn cocktail 58
> Simple beef taco 33
> **Store-cupboard satay** 57
> **Sweet & sour beetroot** 68

M

Madeira cake
> **Salted caramel banana bread** 134
malt loaf
> **Sticky toffee pudding** 130
mango
> **Club tropicana** 129
Marinated courgette, herb & soft cheese 110
marshmallow
> Rocky road s'mores 125
mayonnaise
> **All-day roast** 85
> Buffalo chicken salad 118
> **Cheeseburger toastie** 79
> Mexican chipotle chicken melt 80
> Portuguese sardine 53
> Prawn cocktail 58
> Roast beef Reuben 90
> Toasted club 45
> garlic
> > Brilliant BLT 34
> mustard
> > Toasted club 45
Meatless marinara 50
membrillo
> **Spanish blue** 121
Mexican chipotle chicken melt 80
mint
> **Veggie bahn-miso** 93
> **Veggie tricolour** 75